We Need Insects!

By Anna Prokos

Contents

Introduction

Every day many insects help us
and our planet. Without insects,
Earth would be very different.

wasp

bumble bees

The Earth Needs Insects

Insects are an important part of nature. Some insects help plants grow and others eat harmful insects. Some insects keep the soil healthy. Many insects are food for other living things. Some even make things we use.

▲ **ants**

◀ **Chalkhill blue butterfly**

Some insects can be pests. These insects are harmful to people, plants and other animals. Some pests bite humans and animals. Other pests damage plants. Often, though, these insects are also food for helpful insects and animals.

aphids can damage a plant

brown aphid

green aphid

Insects Help Plants Grow

We need some insects to help plants grow.
Bees fly from flower to flower to sip **nectar**.
When they land on a flower, **pollen** sticks
to their bodies. Then they spread the pollen
as they fly from flower to flower.

bumble bee   pollen

Plants make seeds with the pollen.
Then the seeds grow into new plants.
This way, insects help new fruits,
vegetables and flowers to grow
every day.

pumpkin

watermelon

pear

broccoli

carrots

Insects spread the pollen that helps
fruits and vegetables grow.

Good Insects, Good Eaters

Some insects are helpful to humans. Many of these insects are **predators**. They eat pests.

Ladybirds are great predators. Some ladybirds can eat more than 50 aphids a day. This helps farmers because a group of tiny aphids can damage a whole plant.

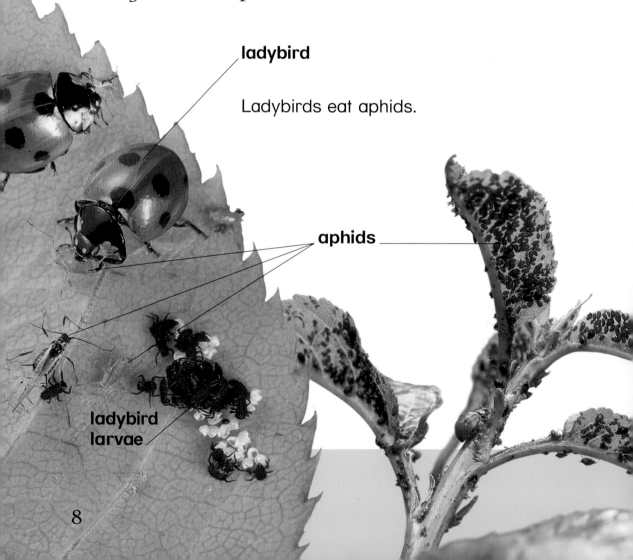

ladybird

Ladybirds eat aphids.

aphids

ladybird larvae

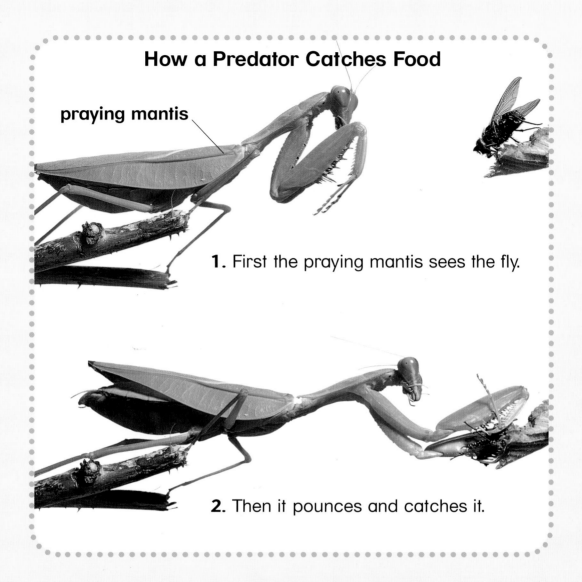

How a Predator Catches Food

praying mantis

1. First the praying mantis sees the fly.

2. Then it pounces and catches it.

Farmers like to have some predator insects
in their fields. That way they don't have to use
as many chemicals to kill pests. These chemicals
can be harmful to people and animals.

Some helpful insects are **parasites** as well. Many parasites lay eggs in pests. Their eggs hatch into **larvae**, or young insects. Then the larvae eat the pest as they grow.

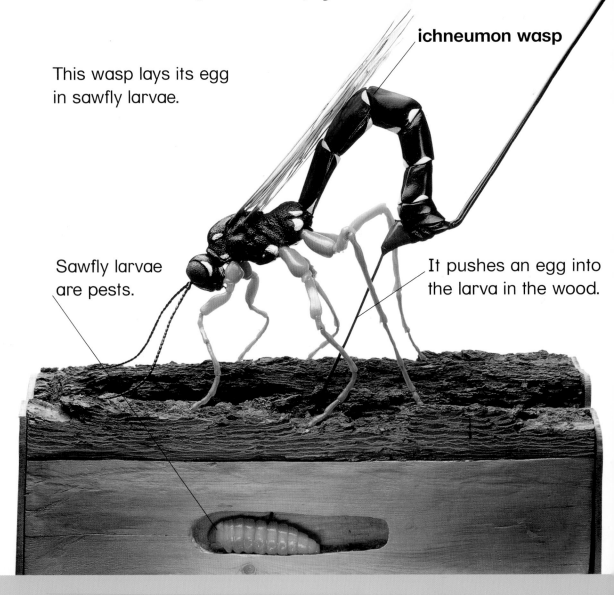

ichneumon wasp

This wasp lays its egg in sawfly larvae.

Sawfly larvae are pests.

It pushes an egg into the larva in the wood.

Marigolds attract hover flies. Hover fly larvae eat pests in the garden.

Clever gardeners find ways to bring helpful insects to their gardens. They attract the insects by growing their favourite plants.

Some helpful insects eat a lot. Lacewing larvae can eat hundreds of aphids in one day. They also like caterpillars and insect eggs. A hover fly larva can eat 50 aphids a day, or up to 400 in its lifetime. An insect called the assassin bug is a hunter. It feeds on many different insects.

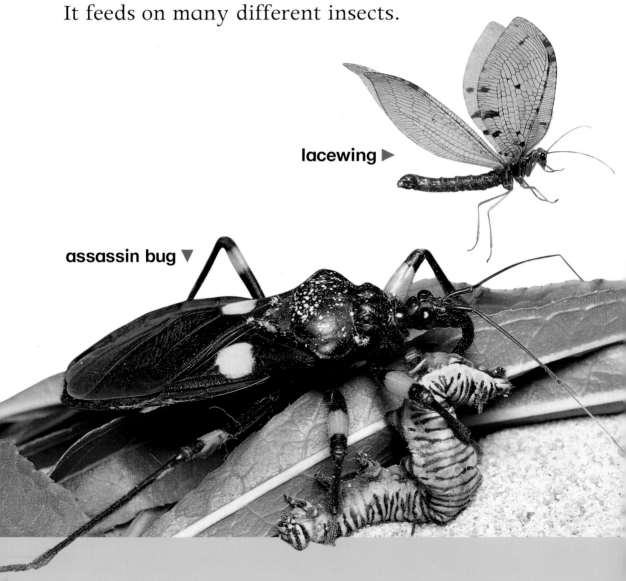

lacewing ▶

assassin bug ▼

Insects Help the Soil

Imagine stepping on dead plants and animals on your way to school. That's what might happen if insects weren't around. **Maggots**, or fly larvae, are **decomposers**.

This beetle is feeding on a bat skeleton.

Decomposers eat dead plants, animals and animal waste. That puts nutrients back into the soil. By doing this, they help make the soil richer.

◄ a group of dung beetles feeding

A dung beetle is a decomposer. It feeds on animal waste. ►

Insects Are Food

Insects are part of a daily meal for many animals. Some birds eat hundreds of insects in one day. Bats and frogs eat insects, too. These animals need insects to survive.

This frog catches a fly with its sticky tongue.

People eat insects, too. In many places people feast on all kinds of insects. Many of these insects are good for you.

▲ tortilla with roasted grasshoppers and avocado from Mexico

◄ This man in Uganda is eating white flying ants.

In Thailand a woman cooks locusts. ▶

Insects Provide Things We Use

Insects help make all sorts of things that people use. Bees make honey for us to eat. **Silkworms** make silk for us to wear. This table shows some products that come from insects.

Products That Come From Insects

Insect	Products
bee	honey beeswax
silkworm	silk
cochineal insects	red dye

Bees Produce Honey

These white cells contain honey.

Bees give us honey. Beeswax from bee hives can be made into candles.

Silkworms Produce Silk

A silkworm makes a cocoon of silk.

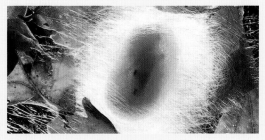

Silk protects the silkworm while it grows.

Insects Are Beautiful

Many people think insects are beautiful.
Some people collect them. Many zoos have
gardens where people can see different insects.

garden chafer beetle

stripe-winged grasshopper

cardinal beetle

mullein moth
caterpillar

seven-spot ladybird

We Need Insects!

What would life be like without insects?
There would be fewer plants. Some plants would be
destroyed by parasites. Dead plants and animals
would decompose more slowly. Some animals might
need to find other food. Next time you raise your
foot to step on an insect, walk around it instead.

Glossary

aphids	tiny insects that feed by sucking sap from plants
decomposers	animals that eat dead plants, animals and animal waste
larvae	young insects that look like worms and caterpillars
maggots	the larvae of a fly
nectar	sweet liquid made by flowers
parasites	animals that live in or on another living thing
pollen	powder made by flowers
predators	animals that kill or eat other animals for food
silkworms	the larvae of a silkworm moth

Index